MIRRORS

REFLECTIONS OF STYLE

MIRRORS

REFLECTIONS OF STYLE

PAULA PHIPPS

W. W. Norton & Company
New York • London

For information about permission to reproduce selections from this book, write to
Permissions, W. W. Norton & Company, Inc., 500 Fifth Avenue, New York, NY 10110

For information about special discounts for bulk purchases, please contact W. W. Norton
Special Sales at specialsales@wwnorton.com or 800-233-4830

Manufacturing by KHL Printing Co Pte Ltd
Book design by Modern Good
Production manager: Leeann Graham

Library of Congress Cataloging-in-Publication Data

Phipps, Paula (Paula Diane)
Mirrors : reflections of style / Paula Phipps. — 1st ed.
    p. cm.
ISBN 978-0-393-70574-4 (hardcover)
1. Mirrors in interior decoration. I. Title. II. Title: Reflections of style.
NK2115.5.M55P49 2012
747'.9—dc23
                                        2011035760
ISBN: 978-0-393-70574-4

W. W. Norton & Company, Inc., 500 Fifth Avenue, New York, N.Y. 10110
www.wwnorton.com
W. W. Norton & Company Ltd., Castle House, 75/76 Wells Street, London W1T 3QT

0 9 8 7 6 5 4 3 2 1

CONTENTS

MIRRORS THROUGH
THE AGES

FROM REFLECTING POOLS TO
ASTRONOMERS' TELESCOPES

The earliest romance to deal with the profound effect of mirrors on our lives is the story of Narcissus, the handsome young hunter of Greek mythology. Disdaining all who longed for his attention, the beautiful youth earned the enmity of the gods for his excessive pride: they made him fall in love with his own reflection in a woodland pool. Unable to tear himself away from the watery image he had fallen in love with, he pined away.

Indeed, the very first mirrors were probably just such pools of still water. After noticing their fluid reflections in ponds and basins, man—and woman—probably next recognized images of themselves in pieces of shiny stone like obsidian, the natural glass produced in volcanic eruptions. Archeologists have turned up what is believed to be the earliest mirrors at Çatal Huyuk (present-day Turkey)—obsidian dating from about 6200 BCE. From that period on, the development and refinement of mirrors have progressed in starts and stops around the world. In Mesopotamia mirrors were crafted of polished copper starting around 4000 BCE; evidence of mirror making shows up in ancient Egypt around 3000 BCE; in China bronze mirrors have been dated as far back as about 2000 BCE, and over the next two millennia, skills to make these desirable objects spread across Africa, Asia and into Europe. The development of glass mirrors changed everything. Mirrors evolved from small handheld objects used in the rituals of beauty to objects large and small.

Today, mirrors contribute beauty, light, space, illusion and sometimes even a sense of history.

1

2

3

4

THE ANCIENT WORLD

[1] The first mirrors were made from natural black glass that resulted from volcanic eruptions. This obsidian mirror from Central America, dated 1400–1500 BCE, and just about the size of an electronic tablet, was highly polished to bring out reflections. Precious obsidian mirrors were part of the treasure trove taken back to Spain three thousand years later by explorers, along with silver and gold, showing the riches of the New World.

[2] A beautiful Egyptian bronze mirror, dating from the Eighteenth Dynasty (ca. 1570–1314 BCE), about 8½ inches high, shows an extraordinary quality of artistry and technique. The handle is in the shape of a woman holding a duck. The details of her face, dress, and the duck are remarkably clear and exquisitely rendered.

This sort of personal item, often buried with the deceased for use in the next life, has been found in many of Egypt's royal tombs.

The Chinese produced beautifully conceived and decorated bronze mirrors used not originally for grooming, but to provide wisdom and guidance from long deceased ancestors. These were given on special occasions, holidays, weddings, and for diplomatic purposes.

[3] This third-century BCE circular bronze mirror from northern China, 9 inches in diameter, depicts dragons on the back and illustrates the sophistication of early Chinese artisans. Chinese metal mirrors were usually highly decorated. They were often buried with the dead to be used in the afterlife, and many survive today.

THE ROMAN EMPIRE

No one knows for sure how or when the making of glass was discovered. But at some point, probably in Mesopotamia around five to eight thousand years ago, someone found that sand, when heated up to a high enough temperature, melted. The addition of potash (the remains of burnt trees) or soda aided in the melting process. Glass naturally has a blue or green tint to it, and glassmakers soon learned that they could alter the colors by adding certain substances.

Although the origins of glassblowing are unknown, by the twelfth to tenth centuries BCE the artisans of Sidon, modern-day Lebanon, were well known for their skill in glass production by various methods and glass making reached its height in the Middle East between 550 and 330 BCE.

By the first century BCE, the Sidon glassmakers had developed the technique of glass blowing.

The ancient Romans learned the techniques of making glass as a result of their conquests (the Romans occupied large areas of the Middle East from about 44 BCE until 476 CE), and the Roman glass industry was well established by the first century BCE. They used bits of metal or molten lead to back glass to enhance its reflectivity, a technique that may have originated in Sidon. [4] A rare glass mirror less than 3 inches high, with a plaster frame, dates from between the fourth and seventh centuries CE. Its iridescent sheen indicates it was buried in sand for an extended period.

Glass mirrors and the use of glass for decorative purposes are mentioned by Roman historian Pliny the Elder (23–79 CE). By that time, Roman writer and philosopher Seneca (ca. 1 BCE–65 CE) could note, "He is truly poor whose room is not lined with a few panes of glass."

The infamous Roman emperor Nero (37–68 CE) decorated his extravagant villa outside Rome not only with marble, ivory, and frescoes but with mosaics that featured bits of glass and mirrors, as well as precious gems on walls and ceilings. (Nero is credited for the innovative idea of putting mosaics on the walls and ceilings rather than limiting them to the floor, creating a glowing, sparking effect all around. However, it was the shiny gold leaf applied to the villa's walls that earned the sprawling collection of buildings its famous name Domus Aurea, the Golden House.)

5   6   7   8   9

The custom of decorating with fragments of glass and tiles began in the Mideast and spread east into India and west through Mediterranean cultures up into southern Europe. In 711 CE, the Moors invaded what is now Spain and remained an important cultural and artistic influence well into the sixteenth century. With them came the tradition of using bits of broken glass, and mirrored mosaics can be found in palaces throughout India.

[5] A spectacular example is this panel from the Seesh Mahal (Hall of Mirrors) in the Amber Fort Palace (begun in 1592) near Jaipur, in Rajasthan. It was built by Raja Man Singh, commander of the Mughal emperor Akbar's army. Thousands of pieces of mirrored glass set in stucco fill the room with light, movement and beauty.

THE MIDDLE AGES

Small handheld metal mirrors made of steel, tin, and other inexpensive metals were not uncommon in Europe. Sometimes a small piece of glass was placed on top of the metal to enhance the reflection. Most people could afford some version of a looking glass.

Early glass mirrors were convex: the glassblower blew a bubble of glass, generally 4 to 10 inches in diameter, the size limited by the glassblower's skill. When the bubble was cut from the blowpipe and cooled, the curved shape was lined with hot lead, which gave a more reflective surface. In some regions the bubble was lined first, then cut. The lead backing made these mirrors fairly dark and although the face and perhaps part of the body could be seen, the reflection was distorted by

the curve.

Sometime during the Middle Ages, glassmakers in Germany and the Netherlands learned to coat the convex glass spheres with tin and antimony rather than lead; in the late fifteenth century, they began to use an amalgam of mercury and lead. The use of such mirrors was recorded in paintings from a later period: [7] *The Moneylender and His Wife*, a 1514 oil on wood by Quentin Metsys (1466–1530), a Flemish artist, incorporates a mirror, popularly believed to be able to identify thieves. And a small convex mirror reflects a woman combing her hair; a male admirer, presumably her husband, looks on [6]. From the sixteenth-century History of Jean III de Brosse and his wife, Louise de Laval, Tours, France.

The first flat mirrors were

produced using a technique developed in the Germanic countries in the eleventh or twelfth century. Artisans blew a bubble of glass, opened it up, and then quickly rotated the blowpipe with the glass still attached. The force of the spin expanded the glass into a flat, circular sheet up to 4 feet in diameter. Once cooled, small rectangular pieces could be cut into rectangles to make windowpanes and small mirrors, but the uneven glass was usually too thin to withstand the hot lead backing needed to create a reflection. Denis Diderot's 1773 Encyclopédie pictures a glassmaker using the crown method to create a flat pane of glass [8].

[9] The cylinder method of glass blowing, a better technique, was developed in the twelfth century, producing larger and more

uniform pieces of glass. It required the glassblower to stand over a pit or on a bench to blow an elongated bubble of glass. When it was the desired size, the glassblower broke it off the pipe, sliced it open vertically along the side, flattened it out on a hot flat metal bed, and reheated it to obtain a smoother, shinier surface and more uniform thickness. Larger, rectangular pieces of glass could be produced. This illustration shows glassmakers in the process of cutting the elongated bubbles.

THE RENAISSANCE

The glass industry flourished in the Renaissance, especially in Germany and Italy. German and Flemish mirror makers started to use an amalgam of mercury and lead to back mirrors. In 1507 Venetian brothers Andrea and Domenico

10

11

12

13

d'Anzolo del Gallo found a way to coat the back of the sheet of glass with an alloy of mercury and tin rather than lead. Not only could the alloy be applied without heat, but it produced an exceptionally bright surface and reflection.

Glass naturally has a blue, green, or brown tint depending on the oxides in the sand used. An enormous step forward in glass production took place around 1450 when Venetian glassmakers developed a recipe for a truly colorless glass, called cristallo for its unprecedented purity. Venice immediately became famous and rich from its production and sale of cristallo for fine tableware and mirrors.

The Venetian glassmaking industry was actually located across the lagoon on the island of Murano, moved there in an effort to

protect the crowded city from the danger of fire from the glassmaker's ovens. But after the discovery of cristallo, the isolated island location had another raison d'etre: guarding trade secrets. So valuable was the cristallo recipe that city officials threatened prosecution of any glassmakers or their families who tried to leave Murano or divulge the secret of making the coveted clear glass. The two technical developments of the colorless glass and the backing with a tin and mercury alloy made Venetian mirrors the most beautiful, the most desired, and the most expensive in the world.

With the improved technology and enhanced beauty of glass, mirrors more and more entered as decorative elements and statement makers. After the death of France's Henry

II in 1559, Catherine de Medici, his Italian wife, had a room filled with more than a hundred prized Venetian mirrors, each reflecting a portrait of the late king that hung in the room.

Mirrors were increasingly visible in many paintings, giving us views of the domestic life of the day. The female nude was also depicted more frequently in painting—usually associated with bathing, and often with a mirror. Artists found mirrors a useful device, allowing them to show multiple perspectives, as well as areas and people outside the scene, all within a single picture. Interesting information can usually be found in these reflections. Over the centuries and up to the present, this artistic concept has been famously used in paintings and later, photographs.

[10] Artist Girolamo

Mazzola-Bedoli used a large mirror to show the beautiful detail of the back of a young girl's dress in this 1542 portrait of Anna Eleanora Santivale.

THE BAROQUE ERA

Around 1617 Sir Robert Mansel was granted permission to establish the first glass factory in England, and in 1663 Englishman George Villiers, the second Duke of Buckingham, persuaded the government to ban imported glass, allowing him to successfully establish his own glass manufactories. The British glass industry had stepped up; soon George Ravenscroft developed a glass recipe that used lead to give the glass a brighter and sharper quality. But France's Louis XIV, the Sun King, led the way in taste and style—and his tastes leaned toward the extravagant. By the 1660s,

his insatiable appetite for all things that sparkled, especially diamonds and Venetian mirrors, was a drain on the royal budget and that of aristocrats who followed suit. Venice's ability to produce fine mirrors and the intense desire for such mirrors by fashionable French citizens put a significant strain on the French economy.

Jean-Baptiste Colbert, Louis XIV's minister of the navy and commerce, limited the import of mirrors, forcing the French to develop and patronize their own mirror industry. In 1665 he established the French Royal Company and enticed some Venetian glassmakers to move to France to help build it up. In 1672 the king purchased seven hundred mirrors from the Royal Company and many were used as lavish promotional gifts to foreign monarchs and

14 15 16 17

dignitaries. Although metal mirrors continued in use, sometimes made of silver or even gold for the wealthy, the increased production of glass caused metal to fall out of fashion for those who could afford glass.

[11] In 1680 French glassmaker Bernard Perrot experimented with casting glass on a flat table made of iron or copper. Now, rather than blowing, molten glass was poured and spread out evenly on a table that was then guided into an oven to reheat. The result was a single pane of glass that could be much larger and have a more consistent thickness than any glass ever made before. Diderot's Encyclopédie illustrates this glassmaking process that allowed production of large sheets of flat glass.

[12] In 1684, the famed Galerie des Glaces (Hall of Mirrors) in the palace at

Versailles was completed. Designed by architects Charles Le Brun and Jules Hardouin-Mansart, the sparkling Galerie des Glaces was designed as a promotional vehicle for the French mirror industry and brilliantly showed off the fine quality of its product. It set off the mania for mirrors in royal and wealthy households throughout Europe and even farther afield, changing the look of aristocratic interiors forever.

The Hall of Mirrors has seventeen false windows and doors that are the same size and design as the seventeen real windows and doors directly opposite. Each of the false windows and doors has twenty-one mirrors for a total of 357, 70 percent of which are original. The real windows open up to the vast gardens, which are reflected in the mirrors and

thus bring the outdoors in. They double the effect of space in the gallery, as well as sunlight by day and sparkling candlelight by night. With this new standard of elegance, royal palaces and aristocratic homes soon had their own public rooms filled with mirrors, incorporated into walls, door panels, and even ceilings, creating rooms designed specifically to impress.

[13] The influence of French design continued. The ground-breaking concept of placing a large mirror above the mantel was introduced in the 1690s, some say by Robert de Cotte, others by Pierre le Pautre. This example is at the Petit Trianon, Versailles. Smaller mirrors were often grouped together to create the illusion of one very large piece of glass, but soon the Royal Glass Company produced the largest mirror

yet. The sheer size—a 9-foot-tall by 3-foot-wide mirror—fueled increasing demands for large mirrors, sometimes covering the whole chimney wall.

The fashion for looking glasses spread worldwide, even to rural homes, and across the Atlantic to America, far from fashion centers. [14] Empress Anna (1730–40) of Francophile Russia officially moved the court from Moscow to St. Petersburg, where the standing residence was redesigned at her request. The epitome of Rococo design, the court included lavish use of mirrors, which is demonstrated here in the boudoir of Empress Maria Alexandrovna in the Winter Palace, St. Petersburg.

[15] The portrait of Mrs. Reuben Humphreys (Anna), an oil painting by Richard Brunton, East Granby, Connecticut, ca. 1799, shows

how many new Americans displayed their prosperity. Here she proudly shows off her most prized possessions—her baby, her porcelain tea set—and her Chippendale-style mirror.

THE NINETEENTH CENTURY

Mirrors were becoming accessible and affordable. In midcentury, England permanently abolished the excise tax on glass. Mirrors had been incorporated into furniture before, but as the prices for mirrors came down and interest in hygiene rose, more were being added to pieces of furniture, and the variety of forms increased [16].

A new method of backing mirror glass using silver was developed by German professor Justus von Leibig. The process, published in 1856, was less hazardous than the toxic

18

19

20

mercury alloy, and provided a stunning reflection. To prevent tarnish, a coating of lead paint was added to protect the silver from exposure to water and air. By the end of the century it was the only process used for the reflective backing of glass for mirrors.

American glassmakers were finally producing mirrors although those who could afford the imported French or English glass continued to buy the European glass because it was considered better quality. Whether domestic or imported, mirrors now provided newly affluent Americans with the opportunity to decorate the palatial houses they were building, houses that sometimes rivaled the European palaces they were copying.

[17] Marble House, the Newport, Rhode Island mansion built by William Vanderbilt, grandson of Commodore Cornelius Vanderbilt, in 1892, illustrates the ostentatious style chosen by the very rich in America at the end of the century. Here, in the Gold Room—the ballroom—an elaborate mirror was built into the paneling above the mantel.

Soon, mirrors would get even bigger. In 1896, an inventor from Pittsburgh, Pennsylvania, introduced a machine that could blow glass cylinders fifty feet long, creating mirrors beyond anyone's dreams.

THE TWENTIETH CENTURY AND BEYOND

As more and more houses became electrified and windows grew larger at the beginning of the twentieth century, mirrors were needed to supplement natural light less and less. But mirrors never completely went out of style. They always provided elegant, glamorous, and increasingly modern architectural elements and accents.

The Art Deco period saw the introduction of large, full sheets of glass, as well as smaller wall mirrors that didn't have frames at all, but beveled edges, emphasizing the sleekness and beauty of glass alone. Furniture with mirrored veneers provided a clean, chic—and expensive — look. Even during the "midcentury modern" era, when exterior walls could be made entirely of plate glass, mirrors continued to play a role, sometimes grand, sometimes quirky.

Thanks to a process developed in 1959 by British manufacturer Sir Allistair Pilkington, mirror making became entirely mechanized, allowing for quantities of glass to be made at a fast pace. Large, flat panes of glass are produced using the float glass process, in which a flow of molten glass floats on top of a constant flow of liquid tin, which doesn't adhere to the glass. The process can run nonstop, twenty-four hours a day for years at a time, and creates a perfectly smooth and shiny surface.

[18] Elegant antique mirrors were still valued diplomatic gifts. On November 2, 1951, Princess Elizabeth presented a seventeenth-century mirror to President Harry Truman, a present from her father King George VI for the newly renovated White House (today it is in the Queen's Room in the White House).

Many decorating trends embrace mirrors. Feng shui—an ancient Chinese belief that choice and placement of architectural features, objects, and colors affect the chi, or energy flow that makes up a person's spirit—considers mirrors crucial for bringing about happiness and good fortune. The "shabby chic" look encourages the mixing of old with new, including old mirrors in modern spaces, or even new mirrors made to look old. Everything old is new again

Mirrors are still a feature essential to dressing and provide a decorative element, disguising doors or enlivening blank walls [19].

[20] Mirrors remain part of our lives, whether we live in a grand home or in a tent. These Bedouin women in Saudi Arabia, who clearly have a certain level of sophistication, improvised a way to hang a mirror even without the existence of solid walls.

→ In a photograph dated ca. 1900, a humorous comment on a custom of the time, the mirror is too high for grooming purposes. The young woman stands on a stool to style her hair as an admirer watches.

REFLECTING ON
HISTORY

HOW MIRRORS HAVE CHANGED OUR PERCEPTIONS OF OURSELVES AND OUR SURROUNDINGS.

Mirrors can be tricky, changing our perception of ourselves and our surroundings and giving us surprising views of things we never noticed outside the looking glass. Not only can mirrors show us who we are, but who we want to be or, at least, how we want to present ourselves. They do more than simply reflect what is set before them. They reflect light—from the sun down to the smallest candle—increasing a room's illumination exponentially. Cunningly placed, they can transform limited space into impressive expanse, produce illusory halls, multiply doorways, even unfurl vistas outdoors.

Mirrors can change our perceptions of the space around us and do something similar for ourselves.

> " Put in lots of mirrors, and then more mirrors, and then more! Indeed I do not think one can have too many mirrors in the dressing room. Long mirrors can be set in doors and all panels, so that one may see one's self from hat to boots."

ELSIE DE WOLFE, *THE HOUSE IN GOOD TASTE*, 1913

They have long played a vital role in our search for acceptance, admiration, and perfection. Rituals of beauty—for special ceremonies, for lovers, for simple vanity—have been practiced in cultures around the world since antiquity.

Probably sometime in the eleventh or twelfth century, artisans learned to make flat glass, enabling the production of large dressing mirrors that could be hung on a wall, held by a servant, placed on a stand, or set on an available table, or covered with a luxurious fabric. Thus the dressing table was born. Here women could create their *grand tenue*—a splendid toilet—applying makeup, styling hair, and adjusting garments. The dressing mirror appeared in a variety of shapes, sizes, and materials. It could make an impressive statement, illustrating status, style, taste, and sophistication. From pocket and hand-held mirrors to mirrors on walls and stands and tables, these looking glasses themselves were meant to be seen and admired. In time, dressing tables became the repository for more and more objects—combs, brushes, and numerous small boxes and bottles.

The ritual of the toilet, which reached its peak in the eighteenth century, generally took place in the boudoir, where aristocratic life played out at an intimate level. Women entertained close friends while "performing" their toilets. French architect Nicolas Le Camus de Mézières (1721–1789) said a boudoir should have plenty of mirrors, including one placed opposite the doorway, so the hostess could easily see who had entered the room, and a mirror above the mantel and on the opposite wall so that she could see herself from every side.

Dressing mirrors evolved from small, portable forms to full-length cheval mirrors to ones incorporated in dressers and vanities that could be either freestanding or built in. The mirrors became objets de vertu—elaborately framed and shaped, on decorated stands. They appear as treasured objects in portraits (and later, in photographs). These recorded images both reveal and conceal. Whether depicting king or commoner, the mirrors are often arranged to show off the owner's prominence and accomplishments.

In the twentieth century mirrors played a role in Hollywood and the entertainment industry, popularizing glitz and inspiring contemporary interiors featuring mirrored rooms and furniture. For ordinary people who would never live a glamorous life, reproducing a similar environment was the next best thing.

← This evocative depiction of an ancient beauty viewing herself in a mirror held by a servant is thought to show the young woman's preparation for marriage. The mural was uncovered in the Villa of the Mysteries just outside Pompeii, where it had been smothered in ash from the eruption of Vesuvius in 79 CE.

↓ A mirror with a support in the form of a draped woman dates from the classical period in Argos Greece, fifth century BCE. Made of bronze, it measures 15-15/16 in. The Greeks are credited for the introduction of free-standing mirrors, an obscure but significant advance in mirror use.

↘ This elegant hand-held mirror case of carved ivory, from the fourteenth century, shows a chivalric tournament. Such mirrors belonged to aristocratic women in medieval France.

← Depicted in a widow's mourning outfit for her husband, Diane de Poitiers (1499–1566), dame de Brézé, Duchess of Valentinois, holds a mirror that hangs from her chatelaine, in a portrait by François Cloet (ca. 1515–1572). Oil on wood.

→ Painter Diego Rodriguez Velazquez (1599–1660) incorporated a mirror, held by Cupid, to allow us a glimpse of Venus's face while we feast our eyes on her exquisitely curvaceous back in this painting of the goddess of love. *The Toilet of Venus* (1647–51), oil on canvas, 122.5 x 177 cm.

⇝ By the sixteenth century, tables were designated specifically for the toilet—the ritual of applying makeup and styling hair. Draped with a heavy cloth or carpet, they typically held easel-like mirrors with glass, as exemplified in *The Woman at her Toilet*, a lithograph by Johann Woelfie after a painting by Gerard Dou.

→ The boudoir of this eighteenth-century aristocratic woman resembled a theatrical set, with the dressing table center stage and laden with toiletry items. Here she would entertain close friends while dressing. A male admirer watches as she is being dressed by her maid. *A Lady Showing a Bracelet Miniature to Her Suitor* is attributed to Jean-François de Troy, ca. 1734.

→→ A painted portrait of Russia's Catherine the Great, by Virgilius Erichsen (Ericksen) shows her in front of an oversized mirror ca. 1762–64. The portrait conveys her dignity and importance, emphasized by the use of her reflected profile in addition to the full-front view of her face.

↘ Two hundred years later, artists and photographers continue to use the mirror in portraits. Queen Elizabeth II of England, ca. 1953, stands before a mirror that reflects an open window.

⇇ Marie Antoinette's boudoir at the Petit Trianon demonstrates an ingenious use of mirrors. By day, the windows open to the luxurious garden. But at night, or when she desired privacy, the mirrors could be raised from a lower floor by a pulley system to completely cover the windows. Here we see them partially raised.

↙ French architect Nicolas Le Camus de Mézières (1721–1789) thought a daybed tucked away in the boudoir was essential. Mirrors should surround it in a niche or alcove to enlarge the space or, with applied decoration, to create an oasis of repose. *The Wall Elevation of a Bedroom Alcove*, ca. 1780, in pen and brown ink, watercolor gouache, and graphite, is by Pierre Ranson (1736–1786).

← An elegant and
expensive silver toilette
set was made in a
collaborative effort by
English craftsmen Jacob
Bodendick, Robert
Cooper, and Andrew
Raven, ca. 1675–1696.

← Mirror frames grew
highly decorated to
complement the beauty
of the glass and the
woman sitting in front
of it. This one, from
seventeenth-century Italy,
is made of walnut with
mother-of-pearl inlay. The
beautiful carving and inlay
continue on the stand.
The glass is a nineteenth-
century replacement.

→ Portable Japanese dressing boxes, like this one pictured in a nineteenth-century Yeizana Japanese scroll print, were traditionally used by actors and geishas. Inside was an adjustable mirror as well as smaller boxes, and several small drawers for toiletries; the form was adapted for European women in the eighteenth century.

↓ An exquisite eighteenth-century dressing mirror from China is filigreed and enameled. Made of silver, wood, silk braid, cut diamonds, and mother-of-pearl, it measures approximately 11 x 22 inches.

↘ A passion for chinoiserie, anything with Chinese design for the western market, swept Europe in the eighteenth century. A dressing mirror based on a Japanese form combined a box with drawers for toiletries and an adjustable mirror, typically hinged. This one, dated ca. 1790–95, belonged to Martha Washington and is finished in black and gold lacquer decorated with floral motifs on gold in geometric patterns—hints of Asian decoration.

→ Chinese porcelain was highly desirable and expensive, leading many European ceramic manufactories to create their own versions. This English Chelsea Porcelain dressing mirror, ca. 1756–58, emphasizes the femininity of rococo curves and floral motifs.

← Another rococo piece is this mirror made by Charles Kandler, ca. 1730s. The Russian Imperial arms and crown surmount the frame, which includes delicate silver flowers, leaves, and other natural forms, including snails and butterflies. As is evident, by now glass could easily be cut into elaborate shapes.

→ This luxurious room, one of the small apartments of Empress Josephine at Fontainebleau (1804–14), is a bathroom: the sofa hides the sunken bathtub. The dressing table is central, its mirror sprouting candle arms. The cheval mirror, also called a psyche, makes an appearance here: its height and adjustability allow the viewer a head-to-toe image. The dressing table is by Thomire, the settee and armchairs by Jacob-Desmalter.

→→ Hepplewhite Rudd dressing table, Mompesson House, Salisbury, England. Dressing tables quickly became a standard form of furniture in every home, sometimes with the mirror attached, sometimes not. Those with multiple mirrors were sometimes referred to as mechanical tables.

← Bathroom of Eugene de Beauharnais (1781–1824), Empress Josephine's son adopted by Napoleon I. The bathroom is lined with mirrors giving reflection upon reflection. Marble encases the zinc bathtub. Hotel de Beauharnais, Paris.

 Shaving- and washstands were introduced in England in the mid-eighteenth century. Below left, an American stand, ca. 1800; below right, a dressing mirror, dated 1830, both plain and decorated only by the grain of the wood.

→ In contrast to the spare pieces on the facing page, this silver, glass, fabric, and ivory dressing table and stool, in the Martelé line produced by Gorham, ca. 1899, demonstrates the revival of the eighteenth-century rococo style favored by many affluent Americans in the second half of the nineteenth century. It was designed by William C. Codman, for Gorham Manufacturing Company, Providence, Rhode Island.

This bronze-and-enamel dressing mirror with an oval glass was made by Tiffany Studios ca. 1900. The peacock-feather motif of the frame was very fashionable at the time, and the connection of the peacock's vanity with the mirror is evident. The feathers spread out to form the base, the epitome of the swirling movement of art nouveau.

→ Marlene Dietrich stands in front of her mirrored dressing table, embodying the theatrical glamour of Hollywood in the 1930s.

↠ Dressing mirror of macassar ebony ivory, and bronze, by Emile-Jacques Ruhlmann (French, 1879–1933, 1919, 14 x 13½ x 5 in.)

← Perhaps the ultimate show-off piece that screamed glitz and glamour is this Baldwin piano, ca. 1976, which belonged to entertainment idol Liberace. Mirrors cover the entire case of the piano, mosaic fashion, reflecting everything around, including, faintly, the pianist himself. Liberace enhanced his over-the-top image with rhinestones and candelabra. He would have given Louis XIV a run for his money.

→ The Amalienburg Pavilion, a hunting lodge at Nymphenburg Palace in Munich, Germany, designed by Francois Cuvilliés and completed in 1739, shows how mirrors could bring the outdoors in. It gives a sense of being surrounded by nature: the mirrors reflect the windows looking out and nature motifs extend up onto the ceiling. Animals, trees, and water, all gessoed and silvered, produce a mystical, cool feeling unlike the traditional gilt.

THE MIRROR
EFFECT

MIRROR-LINED ROOMS ARE DESIGNED TO DAZZLE AND IMPRESS, BUT THEY ALSO HAVE MORE MUNDANE FUNCTIONS.

Lining an entire room with mirrors was clearly meant to astonish and awe viewers, but the practice is not always about making a big impression. There are other, even more functional reasons for the custom. Mirrors expand perceived space, disguise awkward angles and poor proportions, bring the outside in, and—perhaps most important—multiply light, a benefit particularly needed and longed for in the days before electricity.

From roots in the Middle East, the use of mirrors as decorative devices spread around the world, sparking a great love for their beauty and effect. Some of the most spectacular interiors still glow with mirror pieces

"All the interior walls are mirrored, the floors are black marble, and the ceilings have fourteen coats of matte black lacquer. . . . At night, the ceiling and floor seem to disappear, and the mirrored walls reflect the lights. . . . All you can see are lights and stars."

LOYD TAYLOR, DESIGNER, 1978

in elaborate mosaic designs that are as breathtaking now as they were when first built.

Although the French have led the way in fashion and taste since the seventeenth century, and it is they who are credited with raising the bar in terms of what was expected in grand palaces, they were in fact not the first: we can see their forerunners in Persia and India. But once European royalty and aristocrats, wanting to impress each other, began to fill their homes with mirrors, there was no stopping: from the small mirrored cabinet rooms they had installed for contemplative or other purposes to the extensive use of mirrors in wall and door panels, hardly a century went by without some innovation.

In colonial days, American interiors were relatively simple, but as the nation grew, the newly wealthy had the means, if not always the taste, to emulate European aristocrats. By the beginning of the twentieth century, however, a continued interest in mirrors did not result in a simple rehashing of the past; rooms with solid sheets of mirror had a powerful impact, eventually giving way to the modernists, who eliminated walls and the need for mirrors with their glass box houses.

The prosperous 1970s and '80s saw interest in mirrors revive, and in the twenty-first century mirrors have again become fashionable, often with a twist. Instead of flat sheets of glass, decorators create textures, using shards, molded glass, and small mirrored tiles that move, flicker, sparkle, and sometimes cause dizzying effects reminiscent of the time when small bits of mica and glass were used in the mosaics of antiquity, completing another full circle in design.

← Louis XIV's Hall of Mirrors (Galerie des Glaces), in the palace at Versailles, is the mirrored room that started it all. Completed in 1684, it was used for parties and for guests waiting to see the king.

← The Mirror Hall of Golestan Palace, built in Tehran, Iran, during the reign of Tahmasp I, 1524–1576, is an extraordinary example of interior decoration that predates Louis XIV's Hall of Mirrors by a century. The room is lined with mirrors from small to large in a symmetrical design, including a mirrored ceiling on a grid. Although ornate, the design is orderly and grand.

↓ A combination of mirrors and colored glass illuminated by the sun creates a glowing, magical space of warmth and elegance in the City Palace of Udaipur, Rajasthan, India. Construction of the palace, commissioned by Maharana Udai Singh, started in 1559 and continued into the eighteenth century. Breathtaking mirror work is on display in the Palace of Mirrors (Sheesh Mahal), one of the many spectacular buildings that make up the complex.

↑ Completed and decorated between 1740 and 1745, when chinoiserie was the ultimate in European high style, one of the most over-the-top examples of a mirrored room was created at Würzburg Residenz in Würzburg, Germany. The walls are covered with curved mirrors and glass panels framed by gilt molding. The painted panels are verre églomisé, a technique of painting on the back of the glass, either mirrored or not. There are even mirrors on the ceiling. What we see here is a meticulous reconstruction of the original, most of which was destroyed by an air raid during World War II.

→ Across the Atlantic, the Connecticut Room, ca. 1740, is a typical multipurpose room of the American colonial period. Because there were no mirror manufacturers in America until the nineteenth century, mirrors were imported from England or France, sometimes without frames, which could be made and purchased at lower cost. Mirrors were also repaired, resilvered, and updated with new frames.

→→ Peter Zimmerman of Schaefferstown, Pennsylvania, is pictured in his home, proudly showing off his success, his fashionable taste, and a mirror in this watercolor, ca. 1828, by Jacob Maentel. The mate to this portrait shows his wife with yet another mirror.

↑ Illustrations like this one of two windows flanking a mirror, the ensemble with elaborately draped curtains, from Nicholson's *The Practical Cabinet Maker* (1838), were the source for interiors in the "French style" of framing windows and mirror as a unit.

« The large dining room at Mount Vernon, ca. 1785, was George Washington's favorite room. Here, two large, simply framed mirrors placed above matching sideboards were placed on either side of a large Palladian window.

← In Arlington Court, an elegant nineteenth-century English country house in Devon, corner mirrors create their own optical illusion by reflecting each other, tripling any object set in the corner—a good way to enliven a corner or soften an angle.

The Marsden J. Perry home in Providence, Rhode Island, now known as the John Brown House Museum, is an odd pastiche of Palladian, classical, rococo, federal, and chinoiserie elements. The huge mirror on the wall barely fits in the space, but the lavish interior clearly shows that the owner modeled his home on the decor of royal houses. The photograph is undated; Marsden Perry bought the house about 1901.

↓ Anderson House, Washington, D.C., built between 1902–05, is a less ostentatious example of an American Gilded Age idea of an English drawing room. Not all nouveau riche had gaudy ideas of elegance.

↠ The Russian court followed the French with éclat: this nineteenth-century reconstruction of the Armorial Hall of the new Winter Palace in St. Petersburg, built in 1732 and destroyed in a devastating fire in 1837, clearly was modeled on Louis XIV's Hall of Mirrors.

In the middle of the nineteenth century the Maharaja of Jaipur redecorated one of the most spectacular rooms in the seven-story Chandra Mahal, or Moon Palace, in the City Palace in Rajasthan, India. The Shobha Niwas, or Hall of Beauty, was fitted with floral motifs in gypsum covered with gold leaf, the hollow spaces filled with colored tinsel and covered with reflective mica that produced flickering bits of color and light. Large mirrors placed low on the walls reflect the furnishings.

A small, spectacular room originally installed for the personal pleasure of the Maharaja Amarsinhji and connected to his bedroom in Wankaner Palace in Gujarat, India, is completely lined with sheets of mirrored glass, including the ceiling and floor. It was built in 1907–14 and is used as a prayer room today by the current Maharaja.

→ A mirror-lined staircase in the French apartment of style icon Coco Chanel in the early twentieth century is a modern take on luxury.

↠ In a London drawing room designed by Syrie Maugham in 1933, the mirrored wall is actually a screen of vertical mirrored strips that moved.

↓ The concept of "fitted furniture" evolved in the twentieth century—fixed, efficient, and space-saving, like this dressing table with built-in mirror in the master bedroom of Collier's House, seen in the exhibition House of Homes at the PEDAC galleries in New York City, 1940. The architect was Edward D. Stone, the decorator, Dan Cooper.

↓ This room, designed by Ruby Ross Wood in 1937, shows the newfound love of large, flat sheets of glass that can virtually make a wall, or in this case, the fireplace, disappear into space. Mirrors are not just found on the mantelpiece but instead make the full fireplace surround.

← We've seen mirrored ceilings in palatial rooms, and often associate ceiling mirrors with bedrooms, but they can be spectacular in a dining room over the table, where they reflect light and give a full view of the table.

◄◄ A view of a penthouse dining room looking into a living room area in Dallas, Texas, 1979, the creation of design team Loyd Taylor and Paxton Gremillion. Mirrors line the walls and ceilings in bold black-and-white rooms, and large antique mirrors flank the doorway. Loyd Taylor noted that not everyone could comfortably live in such an environment; they would need a "bold personality." The room remains intact today.

◄ Another dramatic Loyd•Paxton interior in the designers' residence in a Dallas apartment building. Black marble floors, black lacquered ceilings, black walls, and an abundance of mirrors and glass walls overlook the city, making the space seem to float in air at night.

← When prohibition ended in the United States in 1933 people began to enjoy the social ritual of cocktails and to install their own home bars, encouraged by Hollywood images. Here movie tough-guy Humphrey Bogart stands behind his home bar; a mirrored background reflects the chic glassware and bottles.

← Home bars, called wet bars when running water is installed, are still common today, even in the most rustic environments, as this contemporary version of rustic and chic demonstrates.

→ Texture breaks up spaces as can be seen in this 1997 interior by Carolyn Corben—a mirrored wall along a set of steps leading up to a mirrored counter and sink area in the bathroom of her own small London flat. The shattered glass yields a kaleidoscope effect.

→→ An outdoor art installation in Tuscany, the Tarot Garden (Il Gardino dei Tarocchi) by artist Niki de Saint Phalle (1930–2002) comprises a group of enormous figures that visitors can walk in and out of. All the interior walls are covered with bits of broken mirror; there are no straight walls or angles, and every inch curves, adding to the overwhelming effect.

The Mirror Effect 63

A bar, stage, stripper pole, and wall of mirrors give a bachelor apartment the look of a club environment. The mirrored wall is a composite of smaller squares, easily installed with adhesive.

← Convex mirrors join to form an oversized screen that adds drama in a New York City apartment.

→ Oversized floor mirrors are a contemporary trend. Here a pair is propped against a wall rather than hung; they give the room a casual yet elegant look.

→ The overmantel mirror was a seventeenth-century French idea that became so popular that it's still a common interior design element today. Before the mantel mirror, fireplaces were heavy architectural elements in a room. The mirror added lightness, literally and figuratively. This example is from a small French boudoir, ca. 1778.

MIRRORS AS
DESIGN
ELEMENTS

MIRRORS DO NOT HAVE TO COVER WHOLE WALLS TO MAKE AN IMPACT. JUST ONE OR TWO CAN DO THE JOB.

Despite the proliferation of mirror-lined walls after the technology to create large, flat mirrors developed, most homeowners did not aim for such extravagance of décor. In fact, just one or two mirrors could produce impressive effects. Often several small mirrors were carefully placed together to give the impression of a large sheet of glass. Looking glasses were usually framed and hung on the wall or built into rooms as part of the architecture. And sometimes they were attached to pieces of furniture.

Architects and decorators who understood just how much reflective glass enhances a space looked for new ways to add mirrors. The pier (the wall

> " If introduced at all in our rooms, the convex mirror must not be regarded as a looking glass ... but simply as an ingenious toy which sets its little panorama going for our mirth, and sometimes redoubles a ray of light. But, it should never 'come in contact with the face.'"
>
> MRS. H.R. HAWEIS, 1881

between two windows) and the expanse above the fireplace became preferred locations, and they remain customary today. Pier mirrors proliferated, and the trumeau, which typically includes a painting above the mirror or an elaborate architectural frame, evolved. The convex mirror made a comeback in popularity: the distorted images they reflected, and the fact that they could show an entire room in miniature, made them novelty items. Some were made in molds that used multiple shapes to produce even more entertaining, fun-house effects. Another development was the plateau: mirrored trays designed to look like a pool of water, reflecting beautiful silver, glassware, and candlelight as well as comestibles.

← Fireplace surrounds and overmantel mirrors quickly became one unit, sometimes extremely ornate. This rococo chimneypiece, ca. 1750, illustrates the lightness of the period and the practice of combining carved wood with marble.

←This seventeenth-century trumeau—a combined mirror and painting—was a gift of England's King George VI to President Harry S. Truman in 1951. It is now in the Queen's Room at the White House.

→ A mirror, dated 1750, at Uppark in West Sussex, England, is attributed to Matthias Lock and is a good example of a pier mirror, practically a form of furniture by this time. Some people did not like placing mirrors between windows because it seemed to create a sense of openness in a place that should be solid. But Nicolas Le Camus de Mézières, a late-eighteenth-century French architect, wrote that imperfect mirrors were often put on the pier wall because the outside light made flaws more difficult to detect. By the nineteenth century, pier mirrors grew in size to be nearly the same size as the windows flanking them. The wall became, in effect, an entire wall of windows and was treated as such.

↓ Mirrors were often set in the fireplace during the summer months when no fires were needed. The reflective glass not only hid the opening but kept warm drafts out of the room. This one is from the Austrian Embassy, in Paris, photographed in 1905 by Eugéne Atget. The camera can be seen in the reflection.

↘ The Saloon at Anton House prominently displays a Queen Anne pier glass, made for the room with beveled Vauxhall plate glass. Beneath it stands a gilt gesso Queen Anne side table.

↓ After receiving an Argand lamp as a gift, in 1790 George Washington purchased over a dozen table lamps and a dozen wall lamps of the improved oil-burning design because they were smokeless, didn't harm the furnishings, and gave more light. Installed in his presidential residence in New York, they went with him when the capital moved to Philadelphia and when he returned to Mount Vernon. This example, the only surviving one, probably came from France and originally was decorated with lacquer japanning.

↓ Brackets and mirrors were often combined to make a lighting device. This is one of a pair of sconces purchased by George Washington, ca. 1791, for his home in Philadelphia, then the capital. They are attributed to Thomas Reynolds. At the end of his presidency, Washington returned to his beloved Mount Vernon and brought them with him.

← With candle arms, mirrors became sconces. This example, ca. 1800–20, is probably English. The fact that the frame is surmounted by an eagle makes it an appropriate ornament for an American home, but this does not necessarily mean it was American-made or made for the American market. The eagle was a common motif in Europe. Today it hangs in the Martha Washington Ladies' Lounge in the Diplomatic Reception Rooms of the U.S. Department of State.

← Convex mirrors made a big comeback in the eighteenth and early nineteenth centuries as novelty items that created amusing reflections. This Regency giltwood-framed mirror from around 1810 shows how the convex shape distorts the reflection but can also capture the view of a larger space and consolidate it.

↙ Convex mirrors were often made in molds, allowing for more entertaining options. In this one, also framed in giltwood, small convex circles make a pattern on the mirror.

↓ A plateau, typically silver or gilt, was a must for an elegant dining room table. This French silver-plate example, ca. 1830, is simple in design.

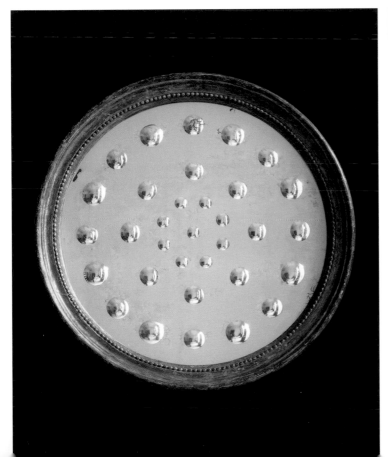

◄◄ Plateaus could come in multiple pieces, to expand as needed. The mirror surface gives a watery effect, reflecting the decorative items placed on top. This lavish one was purchased by President James Monroe for the White House, where it is still used today.

← The breakfast room of architect Sir John Soane, who designed his home as a museum for students to visit and study. An insatiable collector, Soane placed hundreds of mirrors throughout his house to provide interesting views, effects, and light. The breakfast room alone has 100 mirrors, most of which are small and convex. They are placed in the ceiling, along the walls, and in the support beams.

↓ Probably influenced by the French tented rooms like the one opposite, this space was designed to have drapery surrounding what was probably a large convex mirror. The result is the look of a large, bright sun. Design for bed with tented alcove, probably for the Prince of Wales

Bedroom at the Royal Pavilion, Brighton, by Frederick Crace (1779–1859), ca. 1801–404, pen, black ink, brush, and watercolor on white wove paper.

→ Josephine Bonaparte's State Room at Malmaison, 1812, features an overmantel mirror framed by drapery that seems to envelop the room. The tented style, developed around the time of the Napoleonic wars, was originally used in masculine rooms as a reminder of military camps, but soon adapted for more feminine interiors, giving an exotic look.

↑ In an English drawing room, ca. 1885, an overmantel mirror faces a large mirror over a commode, and the two reflect one another; a pier mirror hangs between the windows. For the Victorians, more was more!

◄◄ In a Victorian room embellished with a three-part mirror over the mantel and another, elaborately framed, on the wall behind the sofa, Dante Gabriel Rossetti reads proofs of his sonnets and ballads to Theodore Watts Dunton at 16 Cheyne Walk, London. Gouache, 1882, by Henry Treffry Dunn. By then, the profusion of mirrors could seem outdated: Dunn referred to the room as "one of the prettiest and most curiously furnished old-fashioned parlours . . . mirrors and looking glasses of all shapes and sizes and design lined the walls."

← A collection of unframed art deco–era mirrors hung together adds interest to a plain brick wall in a contemporary loft. The effect of the varied shapes seems more like an art installation than an interior design detail.

→ An imposing piece of Venetian furniture, this tall desk, or secretary, ca. 1730–35, commands attention. Mirrors make this painted, carved, gilded, varnished, and decoupaged piece brilliant. Very thin shelves beneath the cabinet doors pull out, providing a place to set candle stands.

MIRRORED ACCENTS:
FURNITURE

REFLECTIVE FURNITURE
HELPS LIGHT UP ROOMS.

Light has always been a precious commodity. For centuries, only the flicker of burning torches or lamps helped show the way whenever mankind was left in the dreaded dark. Eventually, a different way to aid the benighted was developed. The secret was in reflections that could exponentially increase illumination and pierce the dark.

Very reflective surfaces—silver, brass, highly polished wood, gilt furniture and frames—were keys to brightening up a room. And when mirrors were added to the furnishings, a whole new level of shine and beauty was created. From the sixteenth century onward, mirrors were increasingly used to draw attention

" In Paris people of a particularly amorous disposition sometimes had a plate of mirror-glass set into the domes of their beds, but this practice was less eagerly adopted after Calonne, the Minister of France, was nearly cut in half when the glass fell out of the tester of his bed. The precise circumstances do not seem to be recorded but the Parisians made plenty of jokes about the bed."

ANTOINE CAILLOT, PARIS, 1788

not just to the people in a room but to the room itself and the furniture and objects on display in it.

One of the first pieces of furniture linked to the mirror was the large candle stand, usually placed next to a hanging mirror over a table. Many traditional furniture forms soon had mirrors added to them, including desks, bookcases, cabinets, dressing tables, vitrines, and tables. Pier tables, with mirrors placed against their backs and extending down to the floor, became particularly fashionable. Rather than extending the ceiling and the entire room, such mirrors visually extended floor space and doubled the size of the tables.

The Industrial Revolution fueled the growth of the middle classes and the spread of wealth, producing a profound change in Western culture and lifestyles. New furniture forms—étagères, hallstands, and armoires, with and without mirrors—developed to meet the needs of people who suddenly had enough money to afford some of the niceties of life. Not only the wealthy but also members of the new middle class filled their homes with things to show off their growing sophistication, taste, and prosperity. Some eighteenth-century furniture pieces were made with mirrors, including chairs with mirrors set into their back splats (only a few survive).

In the 1930s and 1940s, the French were once again the instigators of a new look in which objects such as commodes, desks, and tables had mirrors added as veneer. It created a look of high shine and high style and reflected glamour and modernity. Colored mirrors in blues and peaches allowed the furniture to reflect the room without completely disappearing into a maze of colorless glass and helped to create spatial boundaries. It was a trend that did not last long, but it reached far.

The decline in mirrored furniture came with the introduction of new materials such as chrome and polished steel that could produce almost the same reflections as mirrored glass but were cheaper and more durable. This turned the tables on the past: glass had replaced metal; now metal replaced glass!

← This seventeenth-century silver set of table, mirror, and candle stands may not technically be a piece of furniture, but such sets were the forerunners of many forms of furniture that incorporated a mirror. This rare surviving example is in the King's Bedroom at Knole, Kent, England.

→ What looks like an armoire with mirrored doors was, in fact, a bed, made in 1768–70 by Thomas Chippendale for actor David Garrick. The doors of this "cabinet bedstead" opened, and the bed unfolded, an elegant forerunner of the modern Murphy bed. The bed inside no longer exists; it was removed, and the cabinet converted into an armoire.

↓ A mirror-backed "dwarf" bookcase, ca. 1795, is probably by English architect Henry Holland. The reflection would have enlarged the look of the owner's book collection, and perhaps shown off their gilded edges.

↓ This handsome French mahogany dressing table, dated 1787–89, belonged to George Washington—a man who liked fashionable things that were simple and elegant. The top lifts up to reveal the mirror.

↓ A mirror backs this pier table (1800–07) made by English interior designer Thomas Hope for his home, doubling the impact of the decorative legs.

↘ An elegant Federal-style lady's dressing table attributed to William Camp, ca. 1800–10, is an oversized version of the dressing-mirror-with-boxes form. It is highly decorated and features oval glass panels with reverse painting (*verre églomisé*).

A dressing table by the master craftsman Charles-Honoré Lannuier, ca. 1810–19, shows a more masculine form that combines the functions of a commode, dressing table, and mirror all in one.

Rather than prominently placing mirrors on the front of a desk, this fall-front secretary, ca. 1820–25, hides the mirrors inside the case, revealing them only when the desk is opened. This elegant American example of a French furniture form is made of rosewood, omolu, gilded wood, marble, and mahogany.

◄◄ The étagère, or "whatnot," was a new furniture form born during the Victorian period, when a newly affluent middle class accumulated knick-knacks, souvenirs, and mass-produced objects to display.

This rosewood rococo revival piece by Julius Dessoir, ca. 1855, made a splendid setting for these signs of wealth and sophistication.

↓ The posts of the footboard are reflected in two beveled mirrors set into the headboard of the Golden Bed, designed by William Burges for his own guestroom. Made in 1879, the gilded, stenciled, and painted bed illustrates the revived interest in medieval design during the Victorian era.

→ Sideboards grew into enormous structures, often with large mirrors incorporated to emphasize their luxury and importance. This lithograph, from *The Industrial Arts of the Nineteenth Century*, by M. Digby Wyatt, published in 1853, shows a carved oak sideboard by Jackson and Graham that was prominently displayed at the 1851 Great Exhibition in London.

→→ Another exceptional sideboard, known as the Juno Cabinet, by Bruce Talbert, was exhibited in Paris at the 1878 International Exhibition. It is in the Eastlake style, which evolved as a reaction to Victorian excess and is named for architect and writer Charles Eastlake (1836–1906). The mirrors lighten the dark design; strips of wood break up the plain sheets of mirrored glass.

→ This small étagère
by F. & C. Osler, a
high-end manufacturer
known for making
chandeliers, is an
example of the ultimate
in luxury furniture at the
end of the nineteenth
century. To hold the
weight of the glass, the
structure is made of
silvered wood, then
covered with cut glass
and mirrored shelves.

← At the end of the nineteenth century, one could ask if the fireplace-and-mantel ensemble was furniture or architecture. This relatively modest English example, dated 1890–94, was made by an apprentice to demonstrate his skill to qualify for membership in the Guild of Master Cabinet Makers.

→ A magnificent art nouveau cabinet from Castel Béranger in Paris, ca. 1899, is by architect Hector Guimard (1867–1942), best known for his sinuous designs for the Paris Metro entrances. The mirrored glass gives a sense of space within the cabinet.

↠ This art nouveau settee incorporated a mirror, perhaps to reflect the beautiful jewels and necklines of the women who sat on it. The use of mirrors in seating furniture is unusual.

↙ An art deco
commode, ca. 1930,
from the House of
Jansen, an interior
decorating firm that
was based in Paris, is
covered with sheets
of colored mirror, a
style that originated
in France.

↓ A bedroom in India's New Palace (also known as the Art Deco Palace), built 1931–44 in Morvi, in the Rajkot district of Gujarat. Whimsical blue and silver balloon-shape mirrors form head- and footboards. Notice the Venetian mirror on the wall; it adds a touch of old elegance along with the new.

↘ This "Nocturne Radio" (1936) by industrial designer Walter Dorwin Teague (1883–1960) is faced with an art deco–inspired face of cobalt glass, satin chrome steel, and wood.

← An art deco dressing table has become, basically, a large mirror with added drawers in a 1935 design by Robert Block. With its sleek structural look, the design is minimalist in design but not in glamour.

← An angle-fronted sideboard by Graham and Green, ca. 2009, evokes the simple design of the 1950s but with a bold modern touch.

◄◄ This slant-angled dressing table and mirror, ca. 2009, offers a new take on an old form—it could be an art-deco piece.

◄ Today furniture designers are still using mirrors in novel ways to make their pieces stand out. Designer Susan Bruning, also inspired by the mirrored furniture of the 1930s, creates modern mirrored furniture with her own twist. This contemporary cabinet, named Claypool, is covered with mirrors and decorated with floral decoupage. There is no fear of it disappearing into the room.

« An old footstool with a nineteenth-century framed mirror set on top repurposes two less-than-perfect items. Combined, they make a unique and beautiful coffee table in a cozy Alexandria, Virginia, home with Victorian charm.

← Today technology has managed to combine two favorite home furnishings—the mirror and the television. Hidden TV's television would work in almost any room: when it's turned on, it's a TV, but when it's turned off—voilà!—it's a mirror.

→ The discovery of Pompeii and Herculaneum in the eighteenth century prompted a new interest in antiquity. The oval shape of this late-eighteenth-century Russian mirror echoes the patera (shallow offering dish) motif found in classical architecture and was a strong design element in the style of the day. Carved bone and foil give the piece a delicate look.

IN THE
FRAME

FROM SIMPLE TO ELABORATE, FRAMES ADD FINE LOOKS AND PRACTICAL FUNCTION TO MIRRORS OF ALL SHAPES AND SIZES.

Mirrors may keep our secrets, but their frames tell a story. They can offer a glimpse into the times in which they were made as well as the personality of the owner. And no matter when they were made, they speak: "I am rich." "I am modest." "I am vain." Because glass was once so precious, the frame of a mirror had to be worthy of it. And like the setting of a piece of jewelry, frames today can still accentuate the beauty of the glass and all that it reflects.

    Until the twentieth century decorating "rules" dictated that a frame had to be appropriate to the room in which it was placed. Many craftsmen offered their skills to "update" old mirrors: changing the frame was

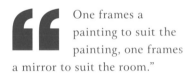
One frames a painting to suit the painting, one frames a mirror to suit the room."

THE SECRET LIVES OF FRAMES,
DEBORAH DAVIS, 2007

eighteenth centuries saw the production of some of the most beautiful designs ever conceived for frames—they were carved out of ebony, pearwood, walnut, cedar, oak, sage, and laurel and enhanced with other luxurious materials, including bone and ivory, colored glass, precious gems, copper and steel, precious metals, simple paint, and expensive gilding.

Today, in a culture that has become so much more casual than that of earlier centuries, there are more design options than ever before. While we have a lingering admiration for sleek elegance, there is also a taste for distressed and rustic looks, for "shabby chic," and even for bare, unframed mirrors, sometimes in unusual shapes.

Whatever their design, mirror frames are still expressions of taste, and mirrors themselves—whether small or large, handheld or wall-hung, framed elegantly and expensively or simply and cheaply—still perform their function admirably, reflecting not just who we are but who we want to be.

a relatively simple and affordable option that that could transform old-fashioned into high style.

Once the technique of making mirrors was perfected, the frame is what was left for creative minds to expand upon. The late seventeenth and early

A sunburst frame with convex mirror illustrates how frames often overshadow the mirror itself.

← This small architectural frame (measuring about 5 x 6 inches), dates from between the fifth and seventh centuries CE and is made of wood decorated with bone plaques. The back is also decorated.

→ A carved walnut Italian tabernacle mirror frame, ca. 1530, is an epitome of Renaissance art, which drew on Greek and Roman models from antiquity. The sides resemble classical pilasters topped by capitals surmounted by molding and a cornice; winged mythological creatures decorate the top and bottom.

← An American mirror typical of a middle-class home of the period (ca. 1825), possibly from New York, has an architectural structure and a top panel of glass that was decorated using the *verre églomisé* technique to depict an important house, local scene, or event. The painting shows a ship docked in the harbor of a New England village. A mirror like this one is seen in the portrait of Peter Zimmerman (see page 47).

→ This fifteenth- to sixteenth- century mirror with carved ivory frame is from Iran. The back side of the frame is elaborately carved.

↠ A frame, ca. 1650–75, is decorated in brightly colored embroidery called stumpwork (three-dimensional needlework with figures raised from the surface). Needlework like this was popular in seventeenth-century England, when it was designed to brighten up dark interiors. It was also a way to illustrate family histories, and at the time of this example, the family's loyalty to King Charles I during the English Civil Wars. The figures here may be Charles I, who was executed in 1649, together with his Queen Henrietta Marie, or Charles II, who came to the throne in 1660, and his consort Catherine of Braganza.

← Figures of cherubs, musicians, dragons, birds, and even a goat nestle amid swirling acanthus leaves in this elaborately carved, dark-stained pine frame, dated ca. 1680–1700. It is an outstanding example of the art put into objects of high value in the baroque period. The mirror is not original.

← This late-seventeenth-century English frame may have been made by Huguenots living and working in England: among the refugee Protestants fleeing from persecution in France were artisans skilled in intricate inlay work.

↑ A gilt oak mirror frame, probably from France, Flanders, or Holland, ca. 1660, has a detachable crest on top. Crests often displayed family insignia or coats of arms. The practice of making the decoration separately may have allowed frames to be more easily updated or to be customized.

↓ Some mirror frames take on a masculine look; others are clearly feminine. This delicate, curving filigree frame from the Netherlands was made of silver wire, ca. 1700, and was probably a woman's dressing mirror. The bow motif, popular in jewelry design at the time, makes an easy transfer to the mirror frame.

↘ A Swedish frame by Gustaf and Christian Precht, ca. 1720–30, is made of narrow strips of mirrored glass painted on the reverse (*verre eglomisé*) with figures including a dancing jester, cherubs, birds, floral sprays, and garlands. The tall crest is of heavily carved gilt wood and painted glass. It's a rare piece.

↓ A German frame, ca. 1710, with a little bit of everything—tortoiseshell, silver, silver gilt, green-stained ivory, filigree, and etched glass—illustrates the metalworking skills of German craftsmen of the time. A piece this elaborate required more than a single artisan, probably at least a cabinetmaker specializing in tortoiseshell and ivory and a silversmith. Johann Valentin Gevers and Johann Andreas Thelot are credited as the makers of this piece.

↓ This exquisite large, engraved glass mirror, possibly from Prague, ca. 1725–50, is one of a pair and shows the influence of Venetian engraved mirror design, which spread throughout Europe as their own industry was diminishing. The frame is made entirely of engraved and pierced mirrored glass with floral motifs surrounding the engraved oval mirror. Bohemian glass making became world famous in the nineteenth century.

↓ An English gilt-wood frame attributed to Thomas Johnson, ca. 1755, shows the freedom designers experienced during the rococo period. Rococo was delicate, curvy, organic, whimsical, and asymmetrical.

↘ As noted earlier, Europeans were enthralled by the exotic East in the mid-eighteenth century. Chinoiserie appeared in furniture, textiles, wallpaper, ceramics— and mirror frames. This mirror is made up of several small pieces of glass, as evidenced by the difference in the condition of the various panels; the frame neatly makes use of the pieces by compartmentalizing them and beautifully disguising the fact that the mirror is not one large piece of glass.

→ This mirror frame by H. F. C. Rampendahl, from Germany, 1860, is made of antlers from two species of deer, boar tusks, and goat horn, all on a wood base. Furniture decorated like this, with full horns and antlers rather than carved or inlaid horn, was fashionable at the time. It was generally relegated to hunting lodges, country homes, and other masculine environments.

→ This work of enameled grisaille on a gold base and blackened wood from mid- to late nineteenth century is by French enamellist Paul Soyer. The technique of enameling on metal refers back to a technique for which France, particularly the city of Limoges, was famous during the Renaissance. Soyer's skill and preference for the classical style and subjects won him numerous medals in all the French World's Fair exhibitions.

↓ Bilbao mirror frames are thought to have originated in Spain, (thus the name), but their true origins remain a mystery. Stylistically classical, the frames are distinguished by the material, usually pink marble applied in narrow strips or in a mosaic pattern. This example, ca. 1800, has added gilt elements, enhancing the already elegant frame.

↓ An American Federal mirror frame, ca. 1800–15, probably from New York, combines the elegant and traditional styles from an earlier Georgian period—the rococo curves and curls at the bottom—with an urn and festoons to create a sort of pastiche.

↘ The style of this American frame, ca. 1800–15, was typical of those made in the area of New York City. The gilding, festoons, balls, and other Federal motifs along with two triangular additions with *verre eglomisé* panels and a large central piece are the identifying elements. The classical-looking scene including a figure is unusual in that the painted scenes usually showed historical themes, landscapes, or maritime images.

↓ An English circular flat mirror with giltwood frame, ca. 1750, has the carved head of Apollo, the Sun God, in the center, emanating his rays. It is one of the early forms of the sunburst mirror.

↘ This Venetian frame from Murano is an example of the nineteenth-century revival of Venetian glass. It exhibits the Victorian era's love of color, flowers, and over-the-top decoration.

→ Sunburst mirrors, like this French example, notable for their frames rather than their glass, came into fashion in the nineteenth century and have remained popular ever since. This one has a convex mirror. It would fit well in almost any décor, from a very traditional environment to sleek art deco to a modern room.

« A beautiful 1922 mirror frame of carved and gilded linden wood by Dagobert Peche, a member of the famed Wiener Werkstätte, has a clean, stylized aesthetic.

↓ An unusual wood-and-stained-glass frame in an art nouveau piece signed "Sarassin." French, ca. 1890.

↘ The cast bronze frame of this standing mirror has the stylized curves so typical of the art nouveau period. The use of cast bronze allowed for such items to be mass-produced with as much or as little detail as desired.

→ Designers Charles
and Henry Greene
helped to create the
American arts and
crafts aesthetic of
"honest" design and
purpose. Plain and
simple, with strong
Japanese influence,
this frame of teak,
ebony, pine, and
leather from 1907 is
a standout.

→→ This frameless mirror,
ca. 1910, was designed
by the eccentric
Spanish artist Antonio
Gaudí (1852–1926) for
the Casa Milà-i-Camps-
La-Pedrera. Its unusual
shape defied what
mirrors were "supposed"
to look like; the beveled
edge acts as a
pseudo-frame.

↘ Today's designers still look to the past for inspiration. Martin Brown doesn't design mirrors to look like antiques but refers to the past through subjects and materials with a new interpretation. The silhouette of this frame echoes the eighteenth century, but the colorful glass mosaic design gives a round mirror a modern and cheerful look.

↘ Many conscientious designers today aim to create designs that aren't meant to look old but do use old or recycled materials. The handsome frame of this mirror, made entirely of rolled up pieces of paper from magazines, is an earth-friendly and colorful work.

→ A mirror on an exterior wall can expand space: this one, in a patio, reflects the garden.

CAPTURING THE
OUTDOORS

MIRRORS CAN EXPAND THE MOODS OF NATURE ITSELF.

For centuries, mirrors were far too precious to be left to the vagaries of Mother Nature and were kept safely indoors. Carefully placed, they could bring the outdoors in by reflecting the gardens outside. Some mirror makers created indoor gardens by painting directly on the glass; painted gardens were in full bloom year round. As mirrors became more affordable and new, sturdy materials were developed, they began to show up outside, placed there by imaginative gardeners and landscape designers. Just as mirrors create the illusions of larger spaces indoors, they enlarge garden spaces; reflections suddenly open up when mirrors are carefully situated against a wall or amid the shrubbery.

" [A] room lined with painted mirrors is really pretty, brilliant and festive, as roses suspended in the air and visited by busy birds or bees, may fairly make it."

MRS. H.R. HAWEIS, "THE ART OF DECORATION," 1881

In urban gardens, where space may be limited, adding mirrors can double the area and create a more open feeling. Many outdoor mirrors have a very architectural feel, with added metal or wood structures creating convincing illusions of gates, passages, or open windows.

Outdoor mirrors are usually made of acrylic or stainless steel—acrylic is lighter in weight and less likely to break than glass. Stainless steel often has a wavy appearance, interesting in itself and especially suitable for fountains. Nevertheless, artists continue to use mirrored glass outdoors in various sizes, functions, and designs. Indoors and out, mirrors continue to delight, entertain, inform, and add a welcome lightness of spirit.

« This mirror (ca. 1710) by French artist Antoine Monnoyer is a rare surviving example of a antique mirror with its original paint, a garden brought indoors.

← In the dining room of a Dallas, Texas, estate, mirrored walls are decoupaged with a variety of plants, flowers, and birds that give the feeling of an outdoor gazebo; the mirrored table in the center, pool-like, adds to the faux garden environment. The design is by Loyd Taylor and Paxton Gremillion.

133

Garden balls, often called gazing balls, have been a popular fixture in gardens for centuries. Over the years, they have accumulated a variety of myths, traditions, and superstitions. Today, they are available in a multitude of colors and sizes; all add a bit of whimsy and sense of magic to a garden.

Placing a mirror on a garden wall can create a very realistic-looking adjacent space. If architectural elements are added to the mirror, as in this faux gate, a secret garden may emerge.

↑ Artist Kate Sell creates weather-resistant mosaics that make stylized flowers grow: here the mirror glass blends into the garden and the poppies seem to be freestanding.

← Enclosed for privacy, this glittering shower stall extends out from a room; it has no ceiling and is completely open to the elements on the island of Lamu, Kenya. Mirrored tiles cover the wall, and when the sunlight and water hit the mirrors, liquid sunshine results, a truly magical look in light and shadow. The house was designed and built by Katy Barker, ca. 2000.

↓ Another artist who brings mirrored mosaics outdoors, Kim Larson uses bits of colored and mirrored glass to decorate and call out the risers of a set of stairs that might otherwise disappear into the surrounding garden.

↙ Here Larson inserts a bit of fun into her landscape design: a jumping frog on a concrete wall adds shine, movement, and humor.

→ *The Garden of Iron Mirrors* by Andrea Stanislav is an outdoor art installation in Minneapolis, Minnesota, with large boulders sided with highly polished sheets of stainless steel that reflect and disappear into the landscape.

ACKNOWLEDGMENTS

Special thanks to all those who provided financial, emotional, and professional support for this project. I couldn't have done it without you:

Brett Alexander, Karen Batra, Bethany Blakey, Lindsay Borst, Robert Kevin Brown, Libby Burton, Amy Carson, Leila Cohen, James and Molly Dickenson, Ranger Due, James Eckman, Lizette Eckman, Steve Garcia, Chris Gavin, Diane Goldenberg-Hart, Nancy Green, Fiona Grimer, Lizzy Griffiths, M. Jeffrey Hardwick, Nancy Hayward, Mark Jordan, Vani Kannan, Kaelie Keating, David King, Gina Lee, Phil McGrew, Tim Mickel, Luis Munoz, John Nestler, Mike Nibley, Carol Phipps, Mark Plants, Susan Riggs, Scott Scholz, Kerry Sessions, Jeff Shuford, George and Jamie Sinks, Alicia Soueid, Emily Thornell, Christine Wagner, Michelle Wagner, Cynthia Williams, Kathy Woodrell

ILLUSTRATION CREDITS

Timeline

1. Obsidian mirror, Central America, 1400-1500 BCE (20.5 X 27.5 X 3 cm). Collection of The Corning Museum of Glass, Corning, New York.
2. Egyptian bronze mirror, 18th century (I I 22 cm). British Museum, London, Great Britain, ©The Trustees of The British Museum / Art Resource, New York.
3. Circular mirror with dragons, Northern China, 3rd century BCE, bronze (H 23 cm). Réunion des Musées Nationaux / Art Resource, New York.
4. Mirror in plaster frame, 4th-7th century, blown glass, plaster frame (H 6.8 cm). Collection of The Corning Museum of Glass, Corning, New York, Gift of Toufic Arakji, 70.1.55b.
5. Detail of a panel with mirrors, Amber Palace. Istockphotos.
6. *Woman Combing Her Hair in Presence of a Gentleman*, from Histoire d'amour sans paroles (history of love without words): History of Jean III de Brosse and his wife Louise de Laval, Tours, France, 16th century, parchment (19X13 cm). Musée Condé, Chantilly, France, Courtesy of Réunion des Musées Nationaux / Art Resource, New York.
7. *The Moneylender and His Wife*, Quentin Metsys (1466-1530), 1514, oil on wood (70.5 X 57 cm). Gérard Blot, photographer, Louvre, Paris, France. Réunion des Musées Nationaux / Art Resource, New York.
8. Denis Diderot, L'Encyclopédie, disbound (bib# 95284). Collection of The Rakow Library of The Corning Museum of Glass, Corning, New York.
9. Denis Diderot, L'Encyclopédie Livourne, Italy, 1773 (bib # 103454) "Glass Souflees" (Pl.36). Collection of The Rakow Library of The Corning Museum of Glass, Corning, New York.
10. *Portrait of Anna Eleonora Sanvitale*, Girolamo Mazzola-Bedoli (c. 1500-1569) 1542. Galleria Nazionale, Parma, Italy, Scala / Art Resource, New York.
11. Denis Diderot, L'Encyclopédie, Livourne, Italy, 1773 (bib # 103454) "Glass, l'Operation de pousser la glace dans la carcaise" (Pl.25). Collection of The Rakow Library of The Corning Museum of Glass, Corning, New York.
12. Hall of Mirrors, Versailles Palace, Versailles France. Paula Phipps, photographer.
13. Petit Trianon, Versailles. Paula Phipps, photographer.
14. The Boudoir of Empress Maria Alexandrovna at the Winter Palace. The State Hermitage Museum, St. Petersburg, Photograph © The State Hermitage Museum.
15. *Mrs. Reuben Humphreys (Anna)* oil painting by Richard Brunton, East Granby, Connecticut, c. 1799. The Connecticut Historical Society, Hartford, Connecticut, gift of the Joslyn Art Museum through Mrs. Frank Willis.
16. Dressing Chest of Drawers, c. 1865-70. Photo by Bruce White, ©White House Historical Association.
17. The Gold Room in Marble House, Newport Rhode Island. David Alan Harvey / National Geographic Stock.
18. Princess Elizabeth presents gift to President Truman, November 2, 1951. National Archives and Records Administration.
19. Istockphotos.
20. Bedouin Women in a Tent. Jodi Cobb/National Geographic Stock.

Chapter 1

Page 12: Woman standing on stool, c. 1900. Snark / Art Resource, New York.

Page 15: Roman Mural painting from the Villa of the Mysteries, 2nd century BCE. O. Louis Mazzatenta/National Geographic Stock.

Page 16, left: Mirror with a support in the form of a draped woman, Greek, mid-5th century BCE, Bronze (H 16"). Bequest of Walter C. Baker, 1971, The Metropolitan Museum of Art, New York, U.S.A., image © The Metropolitan Museum of Art / Art Resource, New York.

Page 16, right: Tournament scene, France, 14th century, ivory mirror case. Museé national du Moyen Âge, Paris, France, Réunion des Musées Nationaux / Art Resource, New York.

Page 17: François Cloet (c.1515-1572) after Portrait of Diane de Poitiers (1499-1566), dame de Brézé, Duchess of Valentinois. Gérard Blot, photographer, Chateaux de Versailles et de Trianon, Versailles, France, courtesy of Réunion des Musées Nationaux / Art Resource, New York.

Page 18: Diego Rodriguez Velazquez (1599-1660), *The Toilet of Venus* 1647-51, oil on canvas (122.5 X 177 cm). Presented by The Art Fund, 1906, National Gallery, London, Great Britain, © National Gallery, London / Art Resource, New York.

Page 19: The Woman at her Toilet, Johann Woelfie, lithograph after Gerard Dou. Stephen A. Schwarzman Building / Art and Architecture Collection, Miriam and Ira D. Wallach Division of Art, Prints and Photographs, New York Public Library.

Page 20: *A Lady Showing a Bracelet Miniature to Her Suitor*, attributed to Jean-Francois de Troy, ca. 1734, oil on canvas, 25 ½" X 18." The Nelson-Atkins museum of Art, Kansas City, Missouri, purchase: William Rockhill Nelson Trust, 82-36/2, photograph by Mel McLean.

Page 21, left: *Portrait of Catherine II in front of a Mirror*, Virgilius Erichsen (Ericksen), 1762-64, oil on canvas (262.5 X 201.5 cm). The State Hermitage Museum, St. Petersburg, photograph © The State Hermitage Museum.

Page 21, right: *Her Majesty Queen Elizabeth II*, Douglas Chandler, c. 1953. Library of Congress.

Page 22: Interior view of the boudoir of Marie Antoinette, Petit Trianon, Versailles, France. Réunion des Musées Nationaux / Art Resource, New York.

Page 23: *Wall Elevation of a Bedroom Alcove*, Pierre Ranson, (1736-1786) c. 1780 pen and brown ink, watercolor, gouache, graphite. Cooper-Hewitt, National Design Museum, Smithsonian Institution, purchased for the Museum by the Advisory Council, 1911-28-263. Matt Flynn, photographer.

Page 24: Toilet Set, c. 1675- 1696, silver, wood, glass, silk and hair, Jacob Bodendick, English, born Germany, active 1661-1688, Robert Cooper, English, active 1664-1717 and Andrew Raven, English, active 1697-1728. Dallas Museum of Art, the Karl and Esther Hoblitzelle Collection, gift of the Hoblitzelle Foundation by exchange.

Page 25: Mirror & mirror stand, walnut frame, mother-of-pearl inlay, with beveled edge glass mirror, Italian, 17th century with glass plate added sometime in 19th century. Victoria and Albert Museum, London, Great Britain, V & A Images, London / Art Resource, New York.

Page 26: Yeizana, Japanese scroll print, 19th century. Victoria & Albert Museum, London / Art Resource, New York.

Page 27, left: Chinese mirror from Russia. The State Hermitage Museum, St. Petersburg, Photograph © The State Hermitage Museum.

Page 27, right: Dressing Mirror, c. 1790-95. Courtesy of the Mount Vernon Ladies' Association.

Page 28: Dressing Table Mirror, Chelsea Porcelain, c.1756-58. Victorian and Albert Museum, London.

Page 29: Mirror with the Russian Imperial Arms and Crown, Charles Kandler, I, England, 1730s. The State Hermitage Museum, St. Petersburg, Photograph © The State Hermitage Museum.

Page 30: Small Apartments of the Empress: view of the bathroom, mahogany washstand by Thomire, settee (on a platform hiding the bathtub built into the ground) and armchairs by Jacob-Desmaler, First Empire, 1804-1814. Gerard Blot, photographer. Chateau, Fontainebleau, France, Réunion des Musées Nationaux / Art Resource, New York.

Page 31, right: Hepplewhite Rudd Dressing Table, Mompesson House, Salisbury. ©NTPL/Peter Cook.

Page 32: Bathroom of Eugene de Beauharnais (1781-1824) Josephine's son adopted by Napoleon I, bathroom with mirrors and wooden columns. Marble bathtub with hot and cold water tap, zinc, Empire, 19th century, Hotel de Beauharnais, Paris, France. Erich Lessing / Art Resource, New York.

Page 34, left: Shaving stand/dressing table, American, c. 1800. Dumbarton House / The National Society of The Colonial Dames of America.

Page 34, right: Dressing Mirror, American, c. 1830. Dumbarton House / The National Society of The Colonial Dames of America.

Page 35, left: Martelé Dressing Table and Stool, William C. Codman, Gorham Manufacturing Company, Providence, RI, silver, glass, fabric, ivory, 1899. Dallas Museum of Art, The Eugene and Margaret McDermott Art Fund, Inc., in honor of Dr. Charles L. Venable, 2000.356.a-b.McD.

Page 35, right: Tiffany Studios, New York, *Dressing Table Mirror,* c. 1900, bronze, enamel, mirrored glass, 18 ½" X 17 ¾" X 7 ¼." Virginia Museum of Fine Arts, Richmond, gift of Sydney and Frances Lewis, photo Katherine Wetzel ©Virginia Museum of Fine Arts.

Page 36: Marlene Dietrich. Mptvimages.com.

Page 37: Emile-Jacques Ruhlman, (French, 1879-1933) Dressing Mirror, 1919, Macassar ebony, ivory, bronze, mirrored, 14" X 13 ½" X 5." Virginia Museum of Fine Art, Richmond. Gift of Sydney and Frances Lewis.

Page 38: Mirrored Baldwin Grand Piano, c. 1976 Serial No. SD21357. Media usage courtesy of the Liberace Foundation for the Performing and Creative Arts.

Chapter 2

Page 40: The Spiegelsaal or glass room, Amalienburg, at Schloss Nymohenburg, Munich, designed by F. Cuvilliers, 1739. Angelo Hornak, photographer.

Page 43: The Hall of Mirrors, Palace of Versailles, 1684. Istockphoto.

Page 44: Mirror room, Golestan Palace, Tehran, Iran. Istockphoto.

Page 45, left: Udaipur Palace, Rajasthan, India. Deidi von Schaewen, photographer.

Page 45, right: Mirror Cabinet at Wuerzburg Residenz. Erich Lessing / Art Resource, New York.

Page 46: Reconstructed room from Connecticut c. 1740. Courtesy Minneapolis Institute of Arts, Gift of Mrs. C.C. Bovey in memory of her mother Josephine Koon.

Page 47, right: *Portrait of Peter Zimmerman*, Jacob Maentel (1763-1863), Schaefferstown, Pennsylvania, c. 1828, watercolor on paper. Collection American Folk Art Museum, New York.

Page 48, left: *The Practical Cabinet Maker*, Peter Nicholson, 1838. Library of Congress.

Page 49, right: The Large Dining Room 1774-1788, George Washington's Mount Vernon, Virginia. Courtesy of the Mount Vernon Ladies' Association.

Page 49: Corner mirrors, 19th century, Arlington Court, Devon, England. ©NTPL / Nadia MacKenzie.

Page 50, left: Marsden Perry House, Providence, Rhode Island, photo c. 1901. Library of Congress.

Page 50, right: French Drawing room, reproduced by permission of The Society of the Cincinnati, Washington, D.C. 2012. ©The Society of the Cincinnati.

Page 51: Armoral Hall at the Winter Palace, St. Petersburg, Russia. iStockphoto.com.

Page 52: Jaipur Palace, Rajasthan India. Deidi von Schaewen, photographer.

Page 53: Prayer room, Wankaner Palace, India. Deidi von Schaewen, photographer.

Page 54: Mirrored staircase in the apartment of Coco Chanel. Victoria and Albert Museum, London.

Page 55: London drawing room designed by Syrie Maugham, 1933. Victoria and Albert Museum, London.

Page 56, left: Collier's House master bedroom, New York, 1940. Gottscho-Schleisner Collection (Library of Congress).

Page 56, right: Mr. Hugh Mercer Walker Residence, New York, NY, living room designed by Ruby Ross Wood, 1937. Gottscho-Schleisner Collection (Library of Congress).

Page 57: Dining room with mirrored ceiling. Istockphoto.com.

Page 58: Dining Room, 19th floor penthouse, Turtle Creek Boulevard, Dallas, Texas, c. 1978, designed by Loyd · Paxton, Inc. Courtesy Loyd · Paxton, Inc. and Loyd Taylor and Paxton Gremillion.

Page 59: Interior of the residence of Loyd Taylor and Paxton Gremillion, 20th floor entry. Courtesy Loyd · Paxton, Inc. and Loyd Taylor and Paxton Gremillion.

Page 60: Humphrey Bogart. Mptvimages.com.

Page 61: Ralph Kylloe, photographer.

Page 52: Carolyn Corben designed sink area, London, 1997. Deidi von Schaewen, photographer.

Page 63: Niki de Sainte Phalle, Tarot Garden, Tuscany, Italy. Deidi von Schaewen, photographer.

Page 64: Paula Phipps, photographer.

Page 65: Deidi von Schaewen, photographer.

Page 66: Deidi von Schaewen, photographer

Chapter 3

Page 58: Paneled Room, 1778, French. Victoria and Albert Museum, London.

Page 70: Rococo chimney and mantel. Victoria and Albert Museum, London.

Page 71: Overmantel Glass with Painting, c. 1695, the Queen's Room, The White House, Washington, D.C. Photograph by Bruce White for the White House Historical Association.

Page 72: Carved gilt wood pier glass, c. 1750, in Red Drawing Room at Uppark, West Sussex. Attributed to Mattias Lock, ©NTPL/Nadia Mackenzie.

Page 73, left: Photograph by Eugène Atget of fireplace in the Austrian Embassy in Paris, 1905. Courtesy Abbott-Levy collection. Partial gift of Shirley C. Burden, The Museum of Modern Art, New York, NY, U.S.A., digital image © The Museum of Modern Art / Licensed by SCALA / Art Resource, New York.

Page 73: Queen Anne pier glass, made for the room with beveled Vauxhall plate glass, Saloon at Anton House. ©NTPL/Andreas von Einsiedel.

Page 74, left: Oval Giltwood Mirror with bracket, c. 1780-90, Mount Vernon, Virginia. Courtesy of the Mount Vernon Ladies' Association.

Page 74, right: Argand wall lamp, probably French, c. 1790, Mount Vernon, Virginia. Courtesy of the Mount Vernon Ladies' Association.

Page 75: Convex mirror with candle arms, English, c. 1800-1820. Courtesy of the Diplomatic Reception Rooms, U.S. Department of State.

Page 76: Giltwood Convex Mirror with gilt frame, c. 1810. Dumbarton House / The National Society of The Colonial Dames of America.

Page 77, left: English giltwood circular frame, 19th century. Courtesy of Carleton Hobbs LLC Collection.

Page 77, right: Table Plateau, French, silver-plate, c. 1830. Dumbarton House / The National Society of The Colonial Dames of America.

Page 78: Plateau, eighteenth-century. The White House Historical Association.

Page 79: Breakfast room. Courtesy of the Trustees of Sir John Soane's Museum, photograph by Martin Charles.

Page 80: *Design for Bed with Tented Alcove*, Frederick Crace, (English 1779-1859), probably for the Prince of Wales Bedroom at the Royal Pavillion, Brighton, c. 1801-04, pen and black ink, brush and watercolor on white wove paper. Cooper-Hewitt, National Design Museum, Smithsonian Institution Museum, purchase through gift of Mrs. John Innes Kane, 1948-40-26. Matt Flynn, photographer.

Page 81, left: The State Room of Josephine Bonaparte, Chateaux de Malmaison et du Bois Préau, Reuil-Malmaison, France, 1812. Réunion des Musées Nationaux / Art Resource, New York.

Page 81, right: Interior of a Drawing Room, c. 1855. Victoria & Albert Museum, London / Art Resource, New York.

Page 82: *Dante Gabriel Rosetti, Theodore Watts-Dunton*, Henry Treffry Dunn, gouache, 1882. ©National Portrait Gallery, London.

Page 83: Collection of Mirrors, interior loft. Deidi von Schaewen, photographer.

Chapter 4

Page 84: Desk, early 18th century (ca. 1730-1735) Pine, carved, painted, gilded, and varnished linden wood decorated with colored decoupage prints, mirror glass, the inside of the fall front lined with silk not original to the secretary (102" X 44" X 23"). The Metropolitan Museum of Art, New York, NY, U.S.A., image © The Metropolitan Museum of Art / Art Resource, New York.

Page 87: Silver set in the King's Bedroom at Knole, Kent, England, 17th century. ©NTPL/Andreas von Einsiedel.

Page 88: Cabinet bedstead by Thomas Chippendale, English, 1768-70. Victoria and Albert Museum, London.

Page 89, left: Dwarf bookcase, probably by Henry Holland, English, c. 1795. Courtesy Carlton Hobbs LLC.

Page 89, right: Mahogany dressing table, owned by George Washington, French, 1787-89. Courtesy of the Mount Vernon Ladies' Association.

Page 90, left: Pier-table, gilt wood, bronze, marble, designed by Thomas Hope for his home in Duchess St. English, 1800-1807. Victoria and Albert Museum, London, Great Britain, V&A Images, London / Art Resource, New York.

Page 90, right: Lady's dressing table, attributed to William Camp, c. 1800-10. Courtesy Maryland Historical Society.

Page 91, left: Dressing table, Charles-Honoré Lannuier, c. 1810-1819. Courtesy of the Diplomatic Reception Rooms, U.S. Department of State.

Page 91, right: Fall-front secretary c. 1820-25, American, rosewood, omolu, gilded wood, marble, mahogany, mirror. Virginia Museum of Fine Arts, Richmond, The Adolph D. and the Wilkins C. Williams Fund, Katherine Wetzel, photographer ©Virginia Museum of Fine Arts.

Page 92: Julius Dessior, (American, born Germany, active 1842-65) Étagère, New York, ca. 1855, rosewood, maple, mirrored glass, brass (63 3/16" X 59 7/16" X 24 13/16"). Cooper-Hewitt, National Design Museum, Smithsonian Institution, Gift of Anonymous Donor, 1937-45-6. Matt Flynn, photographer.

Page 93: William Burges, Bed, 1880. Victoria and Albert Museum, London.

Page 94: Sideboard by Jackson and Graham, exhibited at the 1851 exhibition, London, Lithograph, from *The Industrial Arts of the Nineteenth Century*, by M. Digby Wyatt, published in 1853, shows a carved oak sideboard by Jackson and Graham that was prominently displayed at the 1851 Great Exhibition in London. New York Public Library, Stephen A. Schwarzman Building / Art and Architecture Collection, Miriam and Ira D. Wallach Division of Art, Prints and Photographs.

Page 95: Bruce Talbert, The Juno Cabinet, 1878. Victoria and Albert Museum, London.

Page 96: Osler étagère, glass, wood, mirrored glass, 1885. Courtesy of Mallett & Son Antiques.

Page 97: Fireplace mantle, dated 1890–94, was made by an apprentice to demonstrate his skill to qualify for membership in the Guild of Master Cabinet Makers, © NTPL/John Hammond.

Page 98: Hector Guimard, (1867-1942), cabinet from Castel Béranger, Paris, c. 1899, pear and ash woods, bronze, mirrored glass. Virginia Museum of Fine Arts, Richmond, the Sydney and Frances Lewis Art Nouveau Fun, Katherine Wetzel, photographer, ©Virginia Museum of Fine Arts.

Page 99: Art Nouveau sofa with mirror. Ranza Collection, Parma, Italy, Scala, Art Resource, New York.

Page 100: *Commode,* House of Jansen, French, c. 1930, blue mirrored glass, bronze, giltwood, and gesso (33" x 49"). Dallas Museum of Art, the Patsy Lacy Griffith Collection, bequest of Patsy Lacy Griffith.

Page 101: Bedroom, Morvi Palace, India. Deidi von Scheawen, photographer.

Page 101: Walter Dorwin Teague, American, *Nocturne Radio*, model 1186, c. 1936, mirrored cobalt glass, satin chrome steel and wood (46" x 43" x 12"). Dallas Museum of Art, The Patsy Lacy Griffith Collection, gift of Patsy Griffith by exchange.

Page 102: Robert Block, dressing table, English, 1935. Victoria and Albert Museum, London.

Page 103: Angled Sideboard, c. 2009. Courtesy Graham and Green, London.

Page 104: Slant Angled Dressing Table and mirror. Courtesy Graham and Green, London.

Page 105: Claypool 2, Cabinet, Carson & Co., (www.carsonandco.com) designed by Susan Bruning. Photo by Carson Photography.

Page 106: Living room interior, Alexandria, VA. Paula Phipps, photographer.

Page 107: Mirrored Television, c. 2009. Courtesy of Hidden Television.

Chapter 5

Page 108: Mirror, Russia, late 18th century, bone, glass, foil, carved. The State Hermitage Museum, St. Petersburg, Photograph © The State Hermitage Museum.

Page 110: Collections of the Society of the Cincinnati in the State of New Hampshire at Anderson House, Washington, D.C.

Page 111: Mirror in Wooden Frame Decorated with Bone Plaques, 5th-7th century. 81.1.2, Collection of The Corning Museum of Glass, Corning, New York.

Page 112: Tabernacle mirror, ca. 1530, walnut (29 ¾" X 14 ½"). Robert Lehman Collection, The Metropolitan Museum of Art, New York, NY, image © The Metropolitan Museum of Art / Art Resource, New York.

Page 113: Mirror, c. 1825, possibly New York. Collection of Amy Krupsky, Paula Phipps, photographer.

Page 114: Mirror, 15th-16th century, Iran, ivory. Réunion des Musées Nationaux / Art Resource, New York.

Page 115: Mirror, England 17th century, stump work. Victoria and Albert Museum, London.

Page 116, left: Mirror, c. 1680-1700, dark stained pine, replaced mirror glass (75" X 64" X 4"), Rogers Fund 1967. The Metropolitan Museum of Art, New York, NY, U.S.A. image © The Metropolitan Museum of Art / Art Resource, New York.

Page 117, left: Mirror, England, late 17th century, wood with inlay. Victoria and Albert Museum, London.

Page 117, right: Crested Mirror Frame, c. 1660, oak and gilding (57" X 37" X 7"). Dallas Museum of Art, The Wendy and Emery Reves Collection.

Page 118, left: Mirror, The Netherlands, c. 18th century. Victoria and Albert Museum, London.

Page 118, right: Gustaf Precht, reverse painted mirror in gilded wood frame, Stockholm, Sweden, c. 1720-1730, glass, wood. Collection of The Corning Museum of Glass, (98.31.8) Corning, New York.

Page 119, left: Mirror, c. 1710, Johann Valentin Gevers and Johann Andreas Thelot, German, Oak and pine veneered with tortoiseshell, silver, silver gilt, and green-stained ivory, mirror glass (78 7/8" X 39 3/4"). Wrightsman Fund 1989, The Metropolitan Museum of Art, New York, NY, U.S.A., image copyright © The Metropolitan Museum of Art / Art Resource, New York.

Page 119, right: Engraved glass mirror, possibly from Prague, c. second quarter of the 18th century (65 ¼ " X 28 ¼ " X 2 ½"). Courtesy Carlton Hobbs LLC Collection.

Page 120, left: Giltwood mirror, attributed to a design by Thomas Johnson, English, c. 1755. Courtesy of Carlton Hobbs LLC Collection.

Page 12, right: Mirror, London, England, 18th century. Victoria and Albert Museum, London.

Page 121: Mirror frame, H.F. C. Rampendahl, antlers from two species of door, boar tusks, and goat horn all on a wood base, 1860. Victoria and Albert Museum, London.

Page 122: Paul Soyer, Enamaled mirror frame, c. 1860s, French (31 1/8" X 25 5/8"). Courtesy of Galerie Marc Maison, Paris.

Page 123, left: Bilbao Mirror, c. 1800, wood and marble veneer. Dumbarton House / The National Society of The Colonial Dames of America.

Page 123, center: Looking Glass, c. 1800-1810, probably New York, mahogany veneer, gilt gesso, eastern white pine. Courtesy of the Diplomatic Reception Rooms, U.S. Department of State.

Page 123, right: Looking Glass, c. 1800-1815, New York, New York, eastern white pine. Courtesy of the Diplomatic Reception Rooms, U.S. Department of State.

Page 124, right: English circular giltwood mirror, c. 1750, in the Dining Parlor of The Vyne, Hampshire. ©NTPL / Nadia Mackenzie.

Page 124, right: Venetian Mirror, 19th century, Italian. Douglas Scott photographer for Alhambra Antiques.

Page 125: Sunburst Mirror, 19th century, French, Douglas Scott, photographer for Alhambra Antiques.

Page 126: Dagobert Peche, mirror frame of carved and gilded lindenwood, 1922 (15 ¾ " X 9 ½" [78 X 57 cm]). Neue Galerie New York / Art Resource, New York.

Page 127, left: Mirror frame signed by Sarassin c. 1890, France (59" X 68"). Douglas Scott, photographer for Alhambra Antiques.

Page 127, right: Art Nouveau Mirror, bronze, 19th century. Collection of the author.

Page 128: Green and Green, mirror, 1907, teak, ebony, pine, glass, leather (37 ¾" X 15 7/8" X 1 ¼"). Los Angeles County Museum of Art , digital image © 2009 Museum Associates LACMA / Art Resource, New York.

Page 129, left: Antonio Gaudi (1852-1926) Mirror, c. 1910 (Height .530M). From the Casa Milà-i-Camps-La-Pedrera, photo: R.G. Ojeda, Musee d'Orsay, Paris, France, Réunion des Musées Nationaux / Art Resource, New York.

Page 129, center: Mosaic frame, Martin Brown. Courtesy Martin Brown Mosaicos, Barcelona, Spain.

Page 129, right: Magazine Frame, c. 2008. Collection of the author.

Chapter 6

Page 130: Outdoor mirror. Istockphotos.

Page 132: Mirror, Antoine Monnoyer, c. 1710. V& A Images / Photo Catalogue.

Page 133: Dallas Estate Dining Room with decoupage mirror panels, designed by Loyd · Paxton, Inc. Courtesy Loyd · Paxton, Inc. and Loyd Taylor and Paxton Gremillion.

Page 134: Garden ball. Istockphotos.

Page 135: Courtesy of Fleur Tookey (www.lookingglassgates.co.uk).

Page 136, left: Poppy garden mosaic. Courtesy of Kate Sell of Garden Reflections.

Page 136, right: Tim Beddow, photographer.

Page 137, left: Courtesy of Kim Larson, Mosaic Muralist and Artist (www.kimlarsonart.com).

Page 137, right: Courtesy of Kim Larson, Mosaic Muralist and Artist, (www.kimlarsonart.com).

Page 138: Garden of Iron Mirrors by Andrea Stanislav is an outdoor art installation in Minneapolis, Minnesota, boulders and highly polished sheet of stainless steel. Photography by Kevin D. Hendricks.

INDEX